# How Is Football Made?

Angela Royston

Heinemann LIBRARY

Young Explorer

**www.heinemann.co.uk/library**
Visit our website to find out more information about Heinemann Library books.

To order:
Phone 44 (0) 1865 888066
Send a fax to 44 (0) 1865 314091
Visit the Heinemann Bookshop at www.heinemann.co.uk/library to browse our catalogue and order online.



First published in Great Britain by Heinemann Library, Halley Court, Jordan Hill, Oxford OX2 8EJ, part of Harcourt Education. Heinemann is a registered trademark of Harcourt Education Ltd.



Editorial: Lucy Thunder and Louise Galpine
Design: Jo Hinton-Malivoire and AMR
Illustration: Art Construction
Picture Research: Melissa Allison and Debra Weatherley
Production: Camilla Smith

Originated by RMW
Printed and bound in China by South China Printing Company

The paper used to print this book comes from sustainable resources

ISBN 0 431 05048 1 (hardback)
09 08 07 06 05
10 9 8 7 6 5 4 3 2 1

ISBN 0 431 05055 4 (paperback)
10 09 08 07 06
10 9 8 7 6 5 4 3 2 1

**British Library Cataloguing in Publication Data**
Royston, Angela
How is a football made?
688.7'6334

A full catalogue record for this book is available from the British Library.

**Acknowledgements**
The Publishers would like to thank the following for permission to reproduce photographs: Adidas-Salomon AG pp.**5**, **12**, **13**, **14**, **15**, **16**, **17**, **18**, **20**, **21**, **22**, **23**, **25**; Alamy Royalty-Free p. **28**; AsiaWorks Photography p. **7**; Chris Fairclough Photography Ltd p. **19**; Corbis p. **24** (Walter Hodges); David Wall Photography p.**11**; Getty Images pp. **8/9** (ImageBank), **10** (Stone), **4** (Taxi); Harcourt Education Ltd/Tudor Photography pp. **6**, **26**, **27**, **29**; Science Photo Library p. **28** (Astrid & Hans Frieder Michler).

Cover photograph of footballs reproduced with permission of Harcourt Education Ltd/Tudor Photography.

The Publishers would like to thank Matt Bullock for his assistance in the preparation of this book.

# Contents



Words appearing in the text in bold, **like this**, are explained in the Glossary.

Find out more about how things are made at www.heinemannexplore.co.uk

# What is in a football?

Many children like to play football, especially when they score a goal! Footballs are made in a special way so that you can kick them fast and straight.

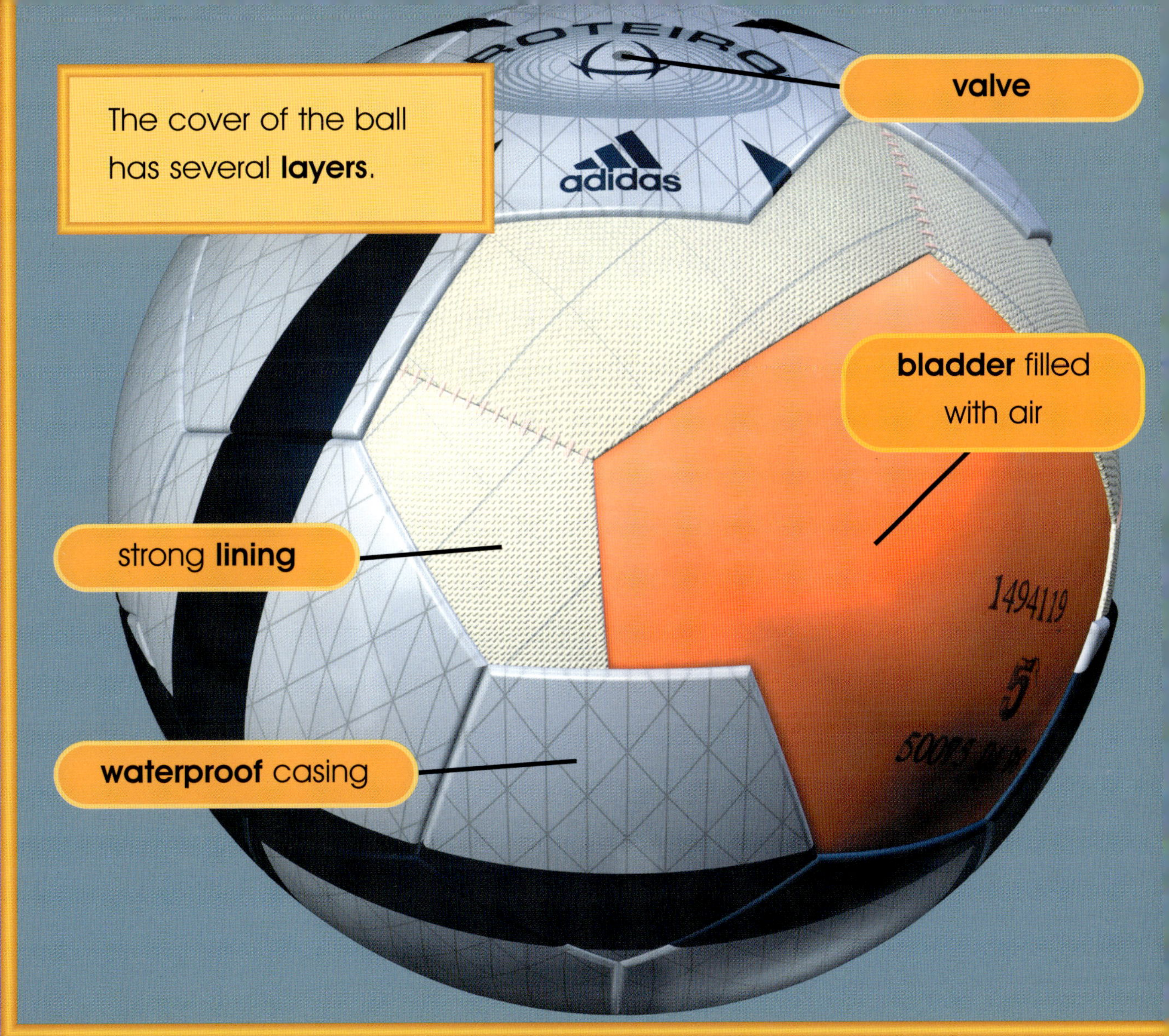


A football is made of **synthetic materials**. These do not wear out even when they are kicked about. The middle of the ball is filled with air.

# Who makes footballs?

Several **companies** design and sell footballs. These companies do not make the balls themselves. They pay factories in other countries to make the balls for them.

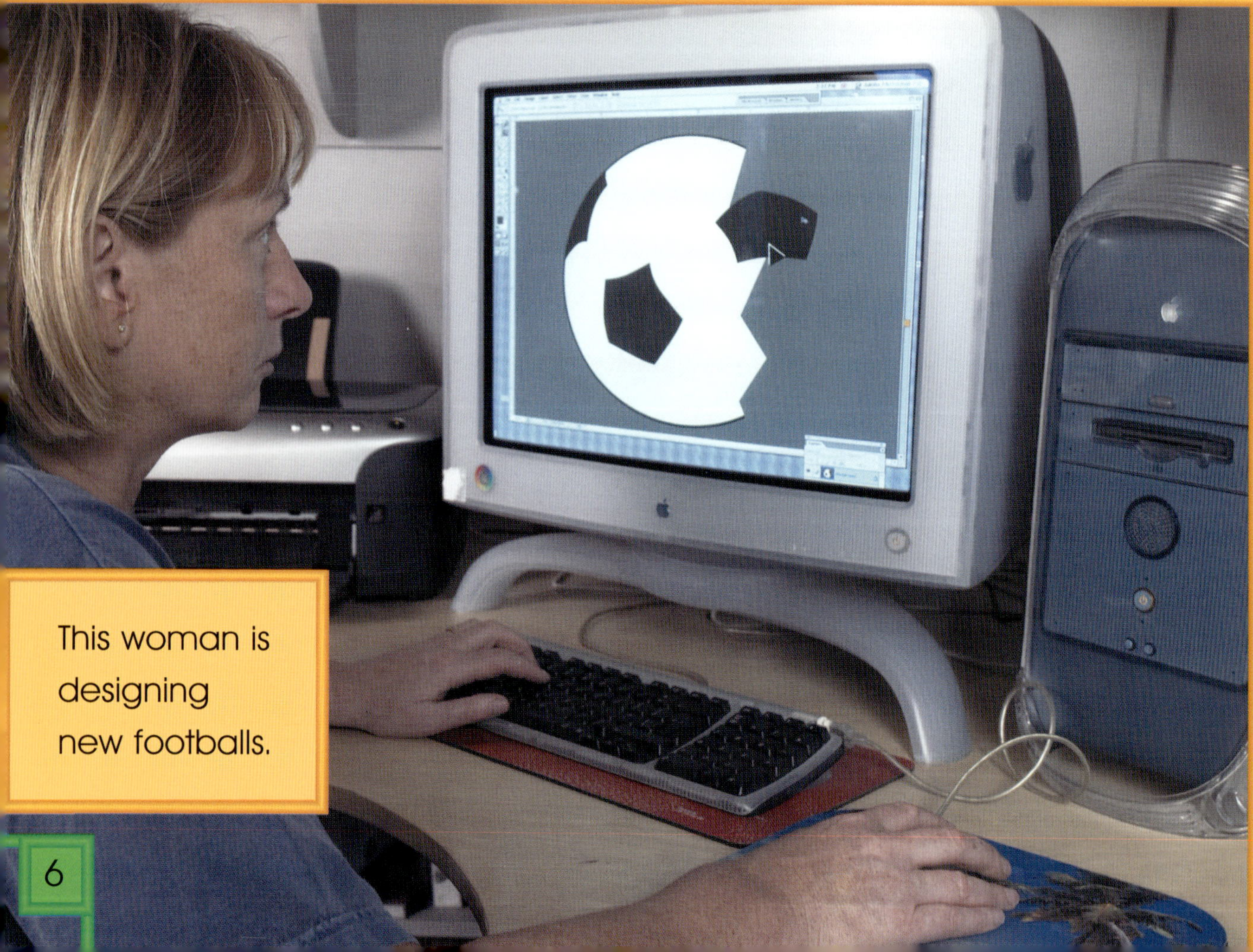

This woman is designing new footballs.

Factories in China, India, and Pakistan pay their workers much less money than workers in Europe and America. This means that the balls cost less to make there.

Many people are needed to make footballs.

# Where do synthetic materials come from?

**Synthetic materials** are made from **oil**. Oil is found deep below the ground. An oil well drills into the ground to reach the oil.

Big ships (called oil tankers) or pipes take the oil to a **refinery**. In the refinery, the oil is separated into petrol and other liquids.

Some oil is brought up from under the seabed.

# Making polyester and PVC

Some petrol is made into plastics. There are many different kinds of plastic. **PVC** is a smooth, shiny plastic. PVC is also **waterproof**.

In the plastics factory a worker checks the machines.

**Polyester** is another kind of plastic. Polyester is made into a strong cloth. Trucks take rolls of **PVC** and polyester from the plastics factory to the companies that make footballs.

# Making the outer casing

The outer casing of the football is made from **PVC**. This helps stop water getting inside the ball. The **layers** in the cover make the ball soft but strong.

**Polyester** or cotton **linings** are glued to the PVC.

The outer cover and linings are dried until they are firmly stuck together. The polyester linings help the ball to keep its shape when it is kicked.

# Cutting the Panels

A cutting machine cuts the cover material into many small panels. Some balls have 26 rectangular panels. Other balls each use 24 hexagons and 8 pentagons.

The cutting machine makes little holes around the edge of each panel. The stitches that hold the panels together will go through the holes.

The different panels for each ball are sorted into piles.

# Printing the Panels

Each panel is printed. The name of the company that designed the football is printed on some of the panels in each ball.

Most companies have a logo. This is a shape or pattern that the company uses on the ball along with its name.

# Stitching the panels

Workers stitch the panels together. It takes around 3 hours to stitch the panels to make a football cover.

The workers stitch the panels together with the cover inside out. They leave the last **seam** open. Then they can turn the cover the right way round and finish the ball from the outside.

# Putting the ball together

Now the cover is ready for the **bladder** to be put inside. The bladder and the cover must be carefully checked.

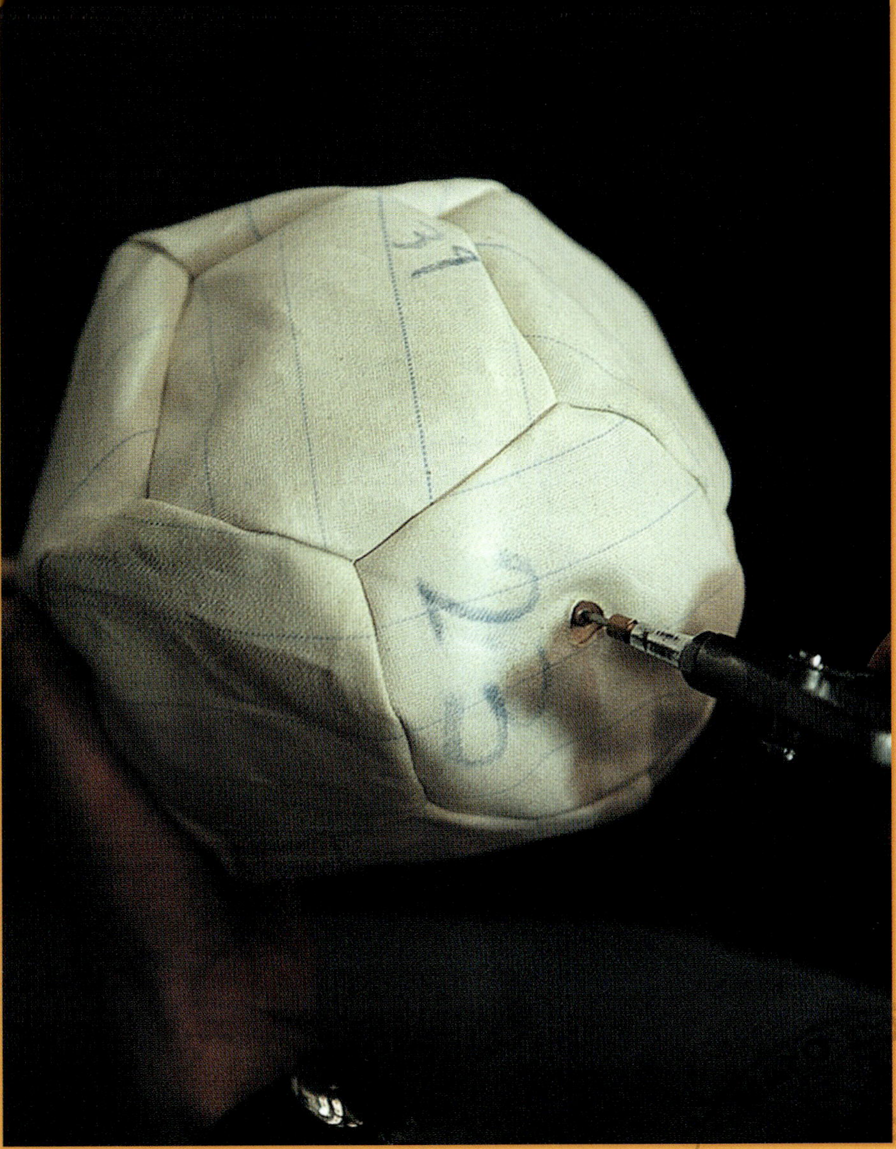



A small hole is cut through the cover and the bladder. The hole is for the **valve**. A special machine puts the valve into the ball.

# Finishing the ball

Air is pumped into the ball to make it round and firm. The **valve** lets air flow into the ball, but stops the air flowing straight out again.

If a football becomes soft, you can pump more air into it.

The air inside the ball makes the ball bounce and fly through the air well. A worker checks the football to make sure it is the right size.

The cover and bladder are also weighed before leaving the factory.

# Packing and storing the balls

Each ball is put inside a clear plastic bag to keep it clean. Lorries and ships take the balls to different countries around the world.

The football **company** stores the balls in its **warehouse**.

When a shop orders some balls, the balls are put in a lorry and taken to the shop.

# Selling the balls

Toy shops and sports shops may sell footballs made by several **companies**. You can look at the different balls before you decide which one to buy.

Some of the money you pay for a football goes to the football company. The company uses it to pay for more balls to be made.

# From start to finish



Footballs are made from plastic, which is made from **oil**.

Workers stitch the cover together from many small shapes.

The bladder is put inside the casing.

Air is pumped into the bladder to make the ball firm and round.

# A closer look



Football covers are made with a range of shapes. The shapes can be rectangles, pentagons, or hexagons.

# Glossary

**bladder** stretchy bag that holds air or liquid

**company** group of people who work together

**cover** outer layer

**layer** single thickness

**lining** material that covers the inside of another material

**oil** liquid that forms under the ground

**polyester** kind of fabric made from plastic

**PVC** tough, bendy kind of plastic

**refinery** place where oil is separated into petrol and other liquids

**seam** row of stitches

**synthetic material** material made from plastics or coal

**valve** gadget that allows something such as air to flow in one direction only

**warehouse** building where things are stored

**waterproof** not letting water soak through

# Places to visit

Catalyst, Widnes: hands-on and interactive exploration of how the science of chemistry affects our everyday lives; *www.catalyst.org.uk*

Eureka! The Museum for Children, Halifax: interactive exhibits exploring the world of science; *www.eureka.org.uk*

Glasgow Science Centre, Glasgow: fun way to learn more about science and technology; *www.glasgowsciencecentre.org*

Magna Science Adventure Centre, Rotherham: science as an adventurous journey; *www.visitmagna.co.uk*

The Science Museum, London: many special exhibitions as well as the museum's historic collection; *www.sciencemuseum.org.uk*

Scienceworks, Melbourne, Australia *www.scienceworks.museum.vic.gov.au*

# Index